FACTS, FIGU ... IOUS GOINGS-ON IN

SHEFFIELD

Tinsley Towers – Sheffield's very own angels of the north that were demolished in 2008. Gone but NEVER forgotten.

FACTS, FIGURES AND FALLACIOUS

GOINGS-ON IN SHEFFIELD

ISBN 978-1-908431-05-9

Published by ACM Retro, 2011

The Grange,

Church Street,

Dronfield,

Sheffield

S18 1QB

www.acmretro.com

That poor narrow place with wood
buildings projecting,

'Twas quite a disgrace;

The roofs nearly meeting, a dark, dreary
street –

Might justly be styled the robber's
retreat,

Where shops were so darkened for want
of true light,

Appeared quite at noontide as though it
was night.

Poet James Wills describes 18th century Church Street.

CONTENTS

Introduction

Chapter One	Famous (or downright infamous) own goals	9
Chapter Two	Crime, punishment and legendary local villains	15
Chapter Three	Speaking Sheffield	21
Chapter Four	Timeline of Sheffield's early history	27
Chapter Five	A guide to notable Sheffield monuments in 1862	33
Chapter Six	Local tragedies	39
Chapter Seven	Sheffield's music heritage trail	49
Chapter Eight	The city on the silver screen	53
Chapter Nine	Sheffield in numbers	57
Chapter Ten	Where to go out in 1879	61

Chapter Eleven	Seven wonders of Sheffield	67
Chapter Twelve	Local legends	71
Chapter Thirteen	Soon to be legends	73
Chapter Fourteen	Where to eat and sleep in Victorian Sheffield	77
Chapter Fifteen	Iconic department stores	79
Chapter Sixteen	Sheffield in the Domesday Book	85
Chapter Seventeen	Where to chill in 1862	87
Chapter Eighteen	Fast facts about our fair city	91
Chapter Nineteen	Football city	93
Chapter Twenty	Did you know ?	95

INTRODUCTION

Sheffield, without a doubt, is one of the best places in the world to live. England's fourth biggest city might have its faults but overall we're pretty together.

Our overriding grit and tenacity has developed from a roller-coaster of an existence that first peaked about the time of the Industrial Revolution when we grew from a small holding-type operation to a Made In Sheffield-style global powerhouse.

We might have had jobs in abundance but squalor-like living conditions left more than a little to be desired and we were regularly seen as the urban blight of Victorian England.

A few benefactors and a few parks later and things started to improve - not least with the opening of our splendid neo-Gothic Town Hall in 1897.

The formation of the legendary Sheffield City Battalion showed our willingness to fight for King and Country in WW1. Sadly our city's brave men will always be remembered as being part of one of the biggest disasters in the UK's military history - the failed Somme offensive of 1916.

The German air force made their first unwelcome visit in September 1916 but nothing could prepare us for the Sheffield Blitz of December 1940 that changed the face of the city forever.

One thing Hitler failed to do was seriuosly dent the steel trade, it took the 1980s recession to do that.

The event made millions for the film industry a decade or so later with the release of The Full Monty, one of the highest grossing films in the history of cinema.

These days we're all Arctic Monkeys and indecision as to whether having a home grown deputy Prime Minister in the shape of Nick Clegg MP was actually a good or bad thing for the city.

So welcome to Sheffield, England's biggest village.

CHAPTER ONE

Famous (or downright infamous) own goals

No city the size of Sheffield could ever hope to thrive without the odd nightmare but we do seem to have a recurring habit of having no one else but ourselves to blame...

If the good Lord indeed loves a trier it's a pretty fair assumption that we're all on a one-way trajectory to the promised land for the following reasons (and there are plenty more where these came from)...

Maradona at Bramall Lane - Eagle-eyed Sheffield United boss Harry Haslam spotted the potential of a certain 17-year-old Diego Maradona playing for Argentinos Juniors way back in 1978. The boss was a renowned for his interest in South American soccer.Reports still differ at the price Haslam had got them down to but one thing's for sure... They missed out on one of the biggest players in the world, opted to pay £160,000 for Alex Sabella instead and were relegated the same season.

Selling Sheffield Airport off for £1 - Nobody can accuse the city of not putting due time and thought into the idea of having an airport – there were calls for one as far back as the 1930s. When it finally opened in 1997 the city was in raptures – Sheffield to Schipol in under two hours and the Steel City was finally an integral part of the global travel hub. Unfortunately the celebrations were short-lived. The meteoric rise in budget flights signalled good news for all airports, bar Sheffield – it discovered its runway wasn't long enough to accommodate the planes. News then filtered out of nearby Doncaster that they were set to open their own - with a big runway. The last scheduled flight left Sheffield in 2002. To add insult to injury the original lease allowed the airport land to be acquired for just £1. A business park now stands in its place.

World Student Games - Few people in Sheffield had heard of the World Student Games before 1991. Now hardly anyone in the city is likely to forget the event or what it has cost. "The very image Sheffield needed to banish, of mismanagement, political turmoil, strikes and disagreements, has returned with a vengeance", Malcolm Pithers - The Independent, 1992. The World Student Games were one of the largest sporting events ever held in the UK but they came at a high cost - far higher than anticipated due to lack of promised Government support, sponsorship that didn't materialise and low ticket sales. On the plus side the city now boasts dazzling sports facilities like Don Valley Stadium and Ponds Forge but the political recriminations and financial headaches are far from over. Mike Bower, leader of the labour-controlled council at the time, said: "The event had the verbal backing of Margaret Thatcher as Prime Minister but the Government failed to offer adequate help towards direct running costs."

National Centre for Popular Music - This was definitely the Lottery funded project that couldn't go wrong. How could it? Everyone loves music and there was even a successful blueprint to follow - Ohio's Rock & Roll Hall of Fame built in an old steel town like Sheffield, Cleveland. Frank Skinner likening it to "a giant Fisher Price toy" signalled the death knell before it had hardly got going... The National Centre for Popular Music was shut within months of opening and the failure knocked the stuffing out of the city's music scene for a good 18 months until the success of the Arctic Monkeys put the sorry, sad affair behind us.

'Threads' - Anyone that had the misfortune to grow up in the Cold War-charged 1980s couldn't have picked a worst place than Sheffield to do it – especially if you weren't adverse to the odd nightmare. The city's backing of 'Threads' – the film that graphically depicted what would happen to Sheffield and its people in the face of a nuclear attack – left an entire generation totally traumatised.

Imitating the Germans - Now there's thinking on your feet and there's thinking on your feet with an American football kit on... The latter definitely muddied the waters as far as common sense was concerned for Steel City's own fledgling team – the Sheffield Spartans. All was looking good at the exhibition match between our homeboys and a team from Munich until, so legend has it, one of the Germans opened their mouths and a distinctly English accent was emitted. 'Munich', it was alleged (and was subsequently splashed across the front of Sheffield's Star newspaper), was actually a motley collection of rookie student American footballers based in the local area that were hastily brought in to fill the gap of a no show by the Germans...

Listing Park Hill Flats - There's no doubt the inner city "streets in the sky" scheme was seen as the saviour of social housing when it was first unveiled in the early 1960s. It allowed the re-housing of an entire community following wide-scale slum clearance. Their ultra-modern design cleverly maintained existing community spirit by re-homing people next door to former neighbours and re-using former street names. Ten foot wide decks even provided enough room for milk floats to deliver door to door. The towering structures take up the bulk of the skyline behind the city's main railway station and stand like a concrete sentinel for anyone entering or leaving the city via one of the main arterial routes, The Parkway. Unfortunately the social housing scheme turned out to be a crime-ridden disaster with the bulk of the estate falling into total rack and ruin and there was only one solution for Park Hill - demolition. But English Heritage had other ideas and, to the total shock of the city, gave them Grade II listed building status in 1998. Over a decade on and the debate still rages – half considering Europe's largest listed building nothing but an eyesore and others believing it to be part of Sheffield's heritage

Demolishing Tinsley Towers - They might have been a pair of unsightly cooling towers by the side of the M1 but they were OUR cooling towers and we loved them. It has to be said that we never heard anyone even mention the 252 foot tall Tinsley Towers when they were standing idle next to Tinsley Viaduct but as soon as the idea of their demolition was mooted they became an overnight sensation that attracted 10,000 to their 3am demolition and sold merchandise by the lorry load. It was definitely our Berlin Wall moment though EON, the site owner, never let anyone onto the site to grab any rubble to auction.

Tree protestors versus the new look Peace Gardens (and proof that some things DO actually turn out okay) - When you look out at the city centre's resplendent Peace Gardens that are now the serene backdrop for weddings/media interviews and everything that's forward-looking about Sheffield you forget the total PR disaster that was looming when work started on the mammoth project. It doesn't take a genius to work out the fact that most people have an affinity with nature and all things green. So sending in a chainsaw gang to cut down an arboretum-style oasis in the middle of the city centre, without prior warning one weekday afternoon, is bound to raise the odd eyebrow. It did – in fact it raised many eyebrows as green activists turned up in their droves to tie themselves to the defenceless trees as the eyes of the media set up vigil in the Peace Gardens. The round-the-clock stand-off carried on for nearly a week. Tempers were running that high following the debacle it divided public opinion around the whole multi-million pound project. Thankfully, when the new-look Peace Gardens were finally unveiled (with more than enough greenery to account for our fallen friends) all was forgotten because everyone loved them.

Meadowhall - Though our very own glitzy out of town shopping Mecca has spread joy to millions right across the region, you have to spare a thought for Sheffield city centre – its retail sector still hasn't recovered, over 20 years since the sprawling mall first opened. Even the 2007 floods – which put great swathes of the place underwater – couldn't give the city centre time to fight back. Meadowhall came back with a refit and another multi-million pound marketing drive. It's all a far cry from the early seventies when such a scheme would have been laughed off the high street. The Sheffield Year Book of 1972-73 proudly stated: "Serving a region of 2,000,000 people, the city's shopping centres are the most modern and attractive in the North. Fifteen big new stores, more than 250 shops, two luxury hotels, two new cinemas, an ice rink, three night clubs and seven multi-storey car parks have been built since the war. "Outstanding in this development is the Castle Square traffic and pedestrian complex. As traffic circles round a great open bowl roundabout, the shoppers below pass from one store basement to another. They can enter the complex from the stores and shops above or by escalators or ramps form the street. Linked into the complex is an extensive system of other pedestrian subways which are planned to segregate pedestrians from road traffic in the city centre and remove the risk of crossing roads. Also linked with the complex is the two-deck shopping scheme in Haymarket which enables shoppers to pass from the Castle Market to the Woolworth Building, one of the biggest in Europe, and to the British Home Stores."

CHAPTER TWO

Crime, punishment and legendary local villains

Sheffield was actually home to one of the most infamous villains in all Victorian England. Charlie Peace was second only to Jack The Ripper in the notoriety stakes.

But you actually have to travel right back to the year 1297 for the city's first official foray into crime and punishment. That was the year Sheffield was granted its Charter and given the green light to hold its very own court on the Wicker (then referred to as 'Sembly Green').

Those in authority were firm believers in people power, even back then, as the locals were given the power to act as judge and jury for more minor offences and act they did.

Justice was doled out via a whipping, a fine or maybe even both. If the menfolk were drunk they had the pleasure of a few hours in the stocks, near the Cathedral, to sober them up.

One of the most heinous crimes back then was 'tippling ' (boozing to you and I) when you should be at church.

But it actually seemed to be the women who received the raw end of the deal – they seemed to have to do little more than open their mouths to get punished.

Punishment for unruly women

The 'cucking stool' which teetered precariously over the side of the River Don near Lady's Bridge was a particular crowd pleaser and a woman only had to be deemed 'unruly' to find herself fastened to the end of the plank and submerged until she nearly drowned.

It wasn't uncommon for the woman, prior to her ducking, to be wheeled around the town to the jeers of the crowd; the method was designed to inflict maximum social humiliation as well as, depending on the mood of who was counting the seconds, near death.

In some circumstances the process could be repeated in short bursts over an entire day.

Unruly married couples could also find themselves bound back-to-back and ducked.

There's also evidence to suggest the 'cucking stool' was regularly carted up town to dole out its torture in Barker's Pool.

The curfew bell

In 1609 the court brought in a rule preventing anyone from 'walking or talking in the street from nine o'clock in the evening till three o'clock in the morning, so as to annoy honest men and householders'. A fine of ten shillings was imposed on anyone who broke the rule. A curfew bell routinely rang at 9pm when everyone went to bed and the day bell followed at 4am, the time for everyone to rise and go to work.

Sheffield's very own gibbet

Up until 1752 capital punishment for thieves and murderers carried out in full view of all comers was thought to be deterrent enough for would be villains. But a new Act of Parliament the same year gave Sheffield the opportunity to up its game and parade the decaying remains for all to see for years on end.

Once wealthy Lincolnshire farmer turned robber Spence Broughton had the pleasure of being hung in chains from the city's own gibbet on Attercliffe Common in 1792 following his execution.

Hundreds turned up to view his body and he ended up suspended for a staggering 36 years.

Capital punishment was doled out faster than the ASBOs of the 21st century back in the good old days. Even Christmas didn't get in the way. A newspaper of December 24, 1820, describes the following sentences given out at the Old Bailey in just a single day:

"Today, 32 persons were sentenced to death, 6 for housebreaking in the daytime, 14 for highway robberies, 4 for burglary, 6, including 3 women, for stealing in dwelling houses, 1 for horse stealing and 1 for sacrilege."

Sheffielders hung in York

The city of York looked after the majority of Sheffielders given the death penalty in the eighteenth and nineteenth century. Crimes of everything from forging banknotes to copulating with animals got a one way ticket to York Tyburn or, after 1801, a portable drop erected at the back of the castle.

Being at the mercy of the hangman wasn't the quick death many would imagine. He was invariably drunk and the slow tortuous strangulation was lapped up by the hundreds that would turn up to enjoy the spectacle.

By 1760 the method of execution saw the condemned person drawn up underneath the crossbeam stood up in a cart. The noose was placed round the neck, the horse whipped and the prisoner left hanging. The drop wouldn't be long enough to break the neck so death wasn't instantaneous.

The hangman might take pity on the victim and pull on their legs to cut short the agony.

On one particular day of multiple executions, the hangman, John Curry, was so inebriated he managed to trip and fall through the trap himself in the middle of the proceedings. He emerged battered and bruised to the hilarity of the crowd.

Bungled executions were commonplace.

The Times, April 4, 1877, said: "As soon as the drop fell, the rope, which was an old one supplied by Askern [the hangman], snapped, throwing the condemned convict Johnson to the ground where he lay groaning. After a delay of about ten minutes a newer and thicker rope was procured and fastened to the cross-beam. Johnson was then led from beneath the drop back on to the scaffold and turned off a second time. This time the rope held and after five minutes of convulsive struggling he expired."

Charlie Peace

No jailbird in the whole history of Sheffield is as infamous as this murderer and career criminal. Charlie Peace's legendary status was second only to Jack The Ripper in Victorian England; he's name checked in Arthur Conan Doyle's Sherlock Holmes tale, 'The Adventures of the Illustrious Client', and became a regular cover star of the 'penny dreadful', the period's sensationalised popular publication. Peace was born in 1832, the son of a one-legged lion tamer.

By 1846 he was crippled himself following an accident at a rolling mill that saw him impaled by a piece of red hot steel that entered his leg just below the knee.

His first foray into crime began as a pickpocket whilst leading a double-life as a virtuoso violinist and popular entertainer.

Charlie Peace made his first appearance in the dock in 1851 when his criminal activities had stepped up a gear – he was charged with housebreaking. He appeared again in 1854 for burglary and by 1876 he tipped the scales of justice with murder.

But it was his constant and persistent evasion of capture via a jaw-dropping mix of disguises, bluffs and double-bluffs that guaranteed his place in the annals of criminal history and Sheffield folklore.

His place as the archetypal Victorian villain even guaranteed a place for him at Madam Tussauds in London.

Sheffield's own mix of hell born bogeyman/swashbuckling daredevil who leapt from a moving train in nearby Kiveton Park to evade capture, was finally led the gallows in 1879.

Gang Wars

The crippling poverty and unemployment that followed in the wake of World War One was blamed for the rise of one of the most vicious and infamous crime waves in the history of Sheffield.

Betting gangs sprung up across the city in the 1920s, praying on punters drawn to the game of 'Tossing Ring': coins held in the flat of the hand and tossed into the air. Bets were laid on the various permutations of heads and tails that landed on the ground.

As revenues increased, with different gangs increasing their stranglehold on different parts of the city, disputes arose and the Sheffield Gang Wars, as they became known, were born.

The city was traumatised as the warring factions brutally fought it out with pitched battles, razor slashing and shootings becoming an everyday occurrence.

The police were totally ineffective at the time with the Chief Constable warning the public that the force was too inadequate to cope.

The gang-charged anarchy ruled the streets of Sheffield from April 1923 to 1925 until the main protagonists were finally brought to justice with two hangings and various prison sentences handed out around September 1925.

POLICE NOTICE.

AMENDED DESCRIPTION OF

CHARLES PEACE,

alias **GEORGE PARKER,** ***alias*** **ALEXANDER MANN,** ***alias*** **PAGANINI,**

WANTED FOR

MURDER

AT SHEFFIELD;

He is thin and slightly built, 46 years of age but looks 10 years older, 5 feet 4 or 5 inches high, grey (nearly white) hair, beard, and whiskers, (the whiskers were long when he committed the murder but may now be cut or shaved off), has lost one or more fingers off left hand, cut mark on back of each hand and one on forehead, walks with his legs rather wide apart. speaks somewhat peculiarly, as though his tongue was too large for his mouth, and is a great boaster.

He is a joiner or picture-frame maker, but occasionally cleans and repairs clocks and watches, and sometimes deals in oleographs, engravings, pictures, &c. Associates with loose women and has been twice in penal servitude for burglaries near Manchester. He has lived in Manchester, Salford, Liverpool, and Hull.

Be good enough to make vigilant enquiries and communicate with

MR. J. JACKSON,
Chief Constable.

CENTRAL POLICE OFFICES,
SHEFFIELD, DEC. 4th, 1876.

[illegible] HIGH STREET AND MULBERRY STREET, SHEFFIELD

CHAPTER THREE

Speaking Sheffield

Many of us thought we'd never see the day a Sheffield accent became a desirable trait for anyone living outside Steel City's seven hills.

But three things ensured we're now one of the most aspirational accents on the planet: Sean Bean, the Arctic Monkeys and The Full Monty.

Back in the bad old days of the 1980s a well-rounded Sheffield drawl almost guaranteed a) the fact you were never going to have a chance of getting any kind of paid employment that involved verbal communication with anyone outside of the city boundary b) you were going to get smacked the moment you opened your mouth in any pub other than those within Sheffield c) your children were going to have little choice but to carry on the Steel City twang tradition as the possibility of attracting a member of the opposite sex with anything other than a Sheffield accent was nil.

So what changed? Why does virtually every TV ad now have a voiceover by Sean Bean or a Sean Bean sound-alike? Why is Sheffield and the South Yorkshire area littered with call centres?

Why do aspiring pop stars think there'll have more chance of landing a record deal if they talk in Arctic Monkey's inspired Sheffield drawl?

Studies have shown that South Yorkshire accents are regularly associated with common sense, loyalty and reliability.

Sheffieldisms that come to international prominence in The Full Monty did - understandably - baffle many of our international friends and there were rumours that many Americans needed an interpreter to help translate the linguistics in parts of one of the highest grossing comedies of all time.

But all too often have we found the annals of phonetic history littered with disastrous attempts at our fair South Yorkshire twang.

Maybe it's because any Sheffielder truly blessed with our fair dialect quickly forgets the years of mentoring he or she has had.

'Research' has pointed to a minimum of four decades in the city coupled with being born into a household of Steel City's finest to even have a prayer of reaching anywhere near the mark.

But, like any global linguistic currency, there are shortcuts and ways to get by on the streets of our fair city so here are a few starters for ten 'mi ol' cock' (my old friend):

Arm – 'arem'

Boots – 'boyits'

Clothes – 'clobber'

Coal – 'coyal'

Very easily upset – 'mardy'

Gentleman – 'mester'

Head – 'ead'

Hole – 'oyal'

House – 'owse'

How – 'ow'

Infant/small child or someone who crys too often – 'babbi'

Light – 'leet'

Mouth – 'gob'

Nose – 'nooers'

Nothing – 'nowt'

Right – 'rete'

Roads – 'Roooads'

School – 'skoyal'

Overly sensitive in the cold – 'nesh'.

Shoes – 'shewus'

Some – 'sum'

Something – 'sumatt'

Please stop it – 'gee'or'

Tonight – 'toneet'

Town – 'tarn'

Washed – 'weshed'

Now you can see from the above that the odd word has the odd rational variation from the accepted English language

– the shortening of the word 'how' to leave 'ow' which wouldn't look out of place in the world of txtspeak today.

The next set of rather longer phrases (or longer phrases condensed into one sledgehammer-type Sheffieldism), which represents a more advanced level, seem to have no rationale whatsoever but are none the less common currency in large parts of Sheffield.

A glossary of this nature is an absolute necessity in many parts of the city.

Are you alright? – 'othaoreet?'

Be quiet please – 'shuthagob'

Could I have a light? – ''as tha gorra lite cock'?

Do you have it with you? – 'asthagoritwithi?'

How does he know? – 'owseeno?'

I haven't heard anything – 'ayanterdnowt'

It is of little or no consequence to me – 'it dunt marrer'

Pass it to the gentleman – 'geeit mester'

Put them in here please – 'pureminere'

Stop crying or I'll you something to cry about – 'gee'orerrur inorI'lgivethisummattorurabout'

What is the matter with you? – 'watsupwidee?'

You are very kind person – 'thasagoodun'

GUNSTONE'S

Ready-cooked

☛ HAMS, ☛

PRESSED BEEF,

Etc.,

For PIC-NICS and

TABLE use. . . . . .

TO BE HAD OF ALL

GROCERS AND PROVISION DEALERS.

BRANCHES:

42, Broad Street,

13, Castle Street,

21, Sheffield Moor.

Do you want to Build a House?

Do you want to Buy a House?

Do you want to Sell a House?

Do you want to obtain a Mortgage on a House? or

Do you want to pay off an already existing Mortgage by small easy instalments?

You can obtain advice and particulars of how to accomplish any of the above by applying to

Mr. R. MITCHELL,

HAYMARKET CHAMBERS, 17 HAYMARKET,

TELEPHONE No. 184. **SHEFFIELD.**

CHAPTER FOUR

Timeline of Sheffield's early history

200AD: Roman legionaries first settle within the manor of Hallam.

450: Hallam ceased to be subject to the Romans.

550: Saxons settle in the area.

828: King Ecgbert of Mercia proclaimed King of England at Dore.

1075: Waltheof, last Saxon Lord of the Manor of Hallam, beheaded.

1110: First Parish Church built.

1183: Beauchief Abbey established.

1264: A visiting party of barons destroy much of Sheffield including the castle.

1270: The second Sheffield Castle is built by Thomas de Furnival.

1297: Furnival's Magna Charta makes Sheffield a free borough. Sheffield becomes a recognised centre of the iron industry.

1408: First Earl of Shrewsbury succeeded by marriage to the Lordship of Sheffield.

1434: Barker's Pool reservoir supplies the town with water

and washes the filth from the streets every month..

1485: Lady's Bridge over the Don is erected in stone.

1510: The Manor House or Lodge is built out of town by the fourth Earl of Shrewsbury.

1530: Cardinal Wolsey detained at Sheffield Manor.

1554: A charter establishes the "Twelve capital burgesses and commonalty of the town and parish of Sheffield".

1570: Mary Queen of Scots brought to Sheffield Castle and placed under the guard of the Earl of Shrewsbury.

1590: Sheffield pen-knives and razors recommended to the "Writing Schoolmaster" for quill cutting.

1604: The Free Grammar School founded on this date.

1624: First Officers of Cutlers' Company appointed under the Act of Incorporation to oversee the town's cutlery trade.

1631: Firm of Marsh Bros. & Co. Pond Steel Works, formed.

1637: 1,000 fallow deer and 200 deer of antler now reside in Sheffield Park.

1642: Sheffield Castle seized by the Cromwellian forces in the Civil War.

1643: The Earl of Newcastle took military possession of Sheffield.

1644: Castle surrendered to the Parliament forces. Parish Church gutted.

1648: Sheffield Castle demolished following an Act of Parliament.

1663: Rev. James Fisher founded the first Nonconformist Society in the city.

1666: The plague ravages nearby Eyam. Constables set "to keep the peste from the towne".

1696: First brick house appears in Pepper Alley. It was "viewed with wonder and ridicule".

1707: The Lord's House (the residence of the Duke of Norfolk) was built in Far Gate.

1713: Sheffield Races take place at Crookesmoor.

1724: Joseph Rodgers & Company Ltd dates from this year.

1726: The building of the Cutlers' Hall.

1736: Sheffield population stands at 14,105. Townhead Cross taken down.

1740: Benjamin Huntsman sets up his factory at Handsworth.

1743: Pinstone Lane Wesleyan Chapel is demolished by rioters.

1746: Two women whipped for stealing linen from a workhouse.

1759: Cutlers' Company start a steel cementing furnace.

1771: Cutlers' Feast becomes a three days' holiday.

1774: Start of William Jessop & Sons, Brightside.

1782: Cutlers' Company are left £8,000 by Thomas Hanbey.

1790: Porch of Parish Church removed.

1792: Spence Broughton executed at York for robbing the Rotherham mail. Body hung in chains on Attercliffe Common (Broughton Lane) for the next 36 years.

1792: Shalesmoor barracks first erected.

1795: Jas. Montgomery, editor of the "Sheffield Iris", gets three months in prison for publishing a song concerning the war.

1800: Manufacture of shear steel begins in the town.

1829: Naylor Hutchinson Vickers & Co. (later Vickers Sons & Co. and now Corus/Tata) founded.

1832: Cholera epidemic kills 402 people.

1836: Botanical Gardens opens.

1840: Firm of Thomas Firth & Sons founded.

1845: Cyclops Works of Messrs. Cammell, Laird & Co. started.

1852: Clyde Steel Works of Osborn & Co. started.

1854: Sir John Brown started the Atlas Works of John Brown & Co.

1855-56: Mr (afterwards Sir Henry) Bessemer invented his steel process.

1864: The devastating Sheffield Flood – 250 lives lost.

1865: Surrey Music Hall burnt down.

1866: Trade Union outrages. Fearnehough, a non-unionist saw grinder, had his house blown up. "Telegraph" agitates for investigation.

1867: Commission enquiry. Murders and outrages, instigated and paid for by William Broadhead, secretary to the Saw Grinders' Union were admitted.

1871: Tom Vickers introduced Siemens regenerative furnace to Sheffield.

1872: Mr (later Sir) Robert Hadfield started Hecla Works.

1875: The Prince and Princess of Wales open Firth Park.

1879: Firth College inaugurated by Prince Leopold.

1885: Sheffield divided into five Parliamentary divisions with five Members. Before Reform Act it had sent two Members to Parliament.

1897: Queen Victoria opens the new Town Hall on Pinstone Street.

1905: Princess Henry of Battenburg unveiled the Queen Victoria Memorial in Town Hall Square. King Edward VII opens Sheffield University.

1908: Sheffield became the centre of the High Speed Steel Trade.

SHEFFIELD SAVINGS BANK,

69, NORFOLK STREET.

ESTABLISHED 1819. CERTIFIED UNDER THE ACT OF 1863.

Open daily—Ten to Three o'Clock; and on Saturday Evening from Five to Seven o'Clock.

BOARD OF MANAGEMENT.

PATRONS :— HIS GRACE THE DUKE OF NORFOLK, E.M.
THE RIGHT HONOURABLE EARL FITZWILLIAM, K.G.

PRESIDENT :—THE RIGHT HONOURABLE EARL OF WHARNCLIFFE.

VICE-PRESIDENTS.

THE RIGHT HONOURABLE EARL OF EFFINGHAM.
THE HONOURABLE W. HENRY WENTWORTH FITZWILLIAM.
THE HONOURABLE FRANCIS DUDLEY STUART WORTLEY.

BAGSHAWE, F. W., Esq.	FIRTH, CHAS. H., Esq.	NEWBOULD, JOHN, Esq.
BARBER, J. H., Esq.	FISHER, WILLIAM. Esq.	ROBERTS, SAMUEL, Esq.
BLAKE, W. GREAVES, Esq.	HARRISON, J. W., Esq.	SORBY, THOMAS A., Esq.
BLAKENEY, Rev. Canon.	HUNT, FREDERICK, Esq.	STEPHENSON, HY., Esq.
CUTLER, JOHN E., Esq.	HOWSON, WILLIAM, Esq.	WALKER, HORACE, Esq.
EARNSHAW, Rev. S., M.A.	LEADER, ROBERT, Esq.	WATSON, H. E., Esq.
ELLISON, M. J., Esq.	MILNER, WM. P., Esq.	WALL, JAMES, Esq.
FIRTH, MARK, Esq.	MOSS, JOSHUA, Esq.	WILSON, THOMAS, Esq.

TREASURER :—WILLIAM WATSON, Esq.

PUBLIC ACCOUNTANT FOR THE YEAR :—NEWMAN H. HUNT.

The number of Depositors on the 20th November, 1878, was 28,925; and the amount due to them was £759,277.

Since the Bank was opened in 1819, £4,654,043 has been deposited, and, including interest, £4,360,497 has been withdrawn by Depositors.

Deposits as small as One Shilling and not exceeding £30 are received during any year, ending 20th November.

Interest is allowed on every Ten Shillings deposited, at the rate of £3 per cent. from the 20th of the month.

The Moneys of the Bank are invested with the Government.

A sum not exceeding Ten Pounds can be withdrawn by the Depositor without Notice, and above Ten Pounds within Seven Days after Notice has been received at the Bank.

Friendly and Charitable or Provident Societies, and Penny Savings Banks may invest all their proceeds, and in case of emergency, can withdraw, without notice, £25.

SUPPLEMENTARY INVESTMENT DEPARTMENT.—Depositors having Accounts of

£200 may transfer £150.
150 ,, ,, 100.
100 ,, ,, 50.

On sums so transferred 3½ per cent. interest is allowed.

Upwards of £20,000 was transferred during the year 1877-78.

GOVERNMENT ANNUITIES for not less than £4, nor more than £50, may be purchased on advantageous terms through this Bank, by annual payments, or by payments in one sum, either immediate or deferred, for life or for a certain term of years. Husband and wife may each have a separate Annuity.

All persons concerned in the management of this Bank are prohibited from disclosing particulars of the register, or the amount of any Deposit, to any person except to the Depositor.

FRANK WEVER, Actuary.

91

CHAPTER FIVE

A guide to notable Sheffield monuments in 1862

As the march of time rolls inexorably on and generations die off, it's easy to forget what monuments we've got (or once had) and what they're actually marking. Here's how our tally was described in 1862:

THE MONTGOMERY MONUMENT. – The memorial to James Montgomery, the poet, stands over his grave at the General Cemetery. It is near the Cemetery-road entrance, the site commanding a beautiful view of the surrounding scenery. It was finished in July, 1861. This interesting memorial was in a large measure the work of the Sunday school teachers and the scholars of Sheffield, who thus testified in the most practical way to the actively religious disposition of the departed bard as well as to his poetic fame. At the unveiling of the statue there was a public procession, in which the Town Council and all public bodies took part. The cost of the statue was £1,000. It was designed by Mr. John Bell, the eminent sculptor, and cast in bronze by the Coalbrook Dale Iron Company. It is a satisfactory work of art, and not unsuccessful as a likeness.

THE CRIMEAN MONUMENT – a monument to the memory of Sheffield soldiers and sailors who died in the service of their country in the Russian war in the Crimea has been erected at Moorhead. The foundation stone was laid by his Royal Highness the Duke of Cambridge. The monument is composed of Darley Dale stone and Aberdeen granite. The granite shaft is 18 feet long, the total height of the monument being about 58 feet. The Statue of Victoria, as "Honour", at the top, is nearly 10 feet high. From £1,300 to £1,400 was collected for the construction of the memorial, but a considerable portion was spent in preliminary expenses. Mr. G. Goldie of London, was the architect, and Mr. Henry Lane, of Birmingham, the sculptor.

THE ELLIOT AND SYKES' MONUMENTS - *There are interesting public monuments in Weston Park in memory of Ebenezer Elliot, the poet and corn-law rhymer, and of Godfrey Sykes, a local artist of reputation. Elliot's monument is a bronze figure on a granite pedestal, the poet being supposed to be seated on a rock in one of the spots so charmingly described in his works. Mr. Burnand, of London, was the artist. The monument was provided by public subscription in 1854, the cost being £600, and stood in Market-place until 1875 when a far more suitable abiding place was found for it among the trees of Weston Park. The name "Elliot" only is inscribed upon it. The monument to Godfrey Sykes consists of a beautifully designed column in terra cotta, placed upon a pedestal of the same material. On one panel of the pedestal is a medallion portrait of the deceased artist, and on the opposite panel a representation of the working tools of the artist.*

THE CHOLERA MONUMENT - *A neat and appropriate monument has been erected on Norfolk-road, opposite the Shrewsbury Hospitals, in memory of those who died in Sheffield from the ravages of cholera in 1832 and who were buried on this spot. The disease raged from the beginning of July till the end of October. The numbers attacked were 1,347, of whom 402 died. Amongst the victims was Mr. John Blake, the master cutler. The monument was erected in 1834-5, the corner stone having been laid by Montgomery, the poet, in December of the former year.*

The Crimean monument that was standing proudly at Moorhead in days gone by

A list of early Sheffield newspapers:

Lister's Sheffield Weekly Journal - established 1754.

Sheffield Weekly Register - established 1755.

Sheffield Public Advertiser - established 1770.

Sheffield Register - established 1787.

Sheffield Iris - established 1794.

Sheffield Mercury - established 1807.

Sheffield Independent & Commercial Register - established 1819.

Sheffield Courant - established 1827.

Sheffield & Rotherham Independent - established 1839.

Lady's Bridge in 1879

This legendary crossing was beginning to fall out of public consciousness until Richard Hawley brought it back to the fore with his album of the same name. The Victorians were big fans and it regularly made the pages of Sheffield guide books of the era. Here's how it was described in 1879:

"One of the oldest structures in the town is Lady's Bridge – the connecting link between Waingate and the Wicker. The original bridge was, without a doubt, in existence in the time of Henry II., and was, therefore, probably built at the same time as the castle of the De Lovetots, at the foot of which it stood. It was rebuilt in a very substantial way during the reign of Henry VII. It has been lately widened by the Town Council, but without any disturbance of the old structure. Its name was derived from a small chapel dedicated to "Our Lady", which formerly stood at the west end of the bridge under the castle wall."

The Richardson
8-10 H.P.
Sporting 2-3 Seater
LIGHT CAR
GUARANTEED PETROL CONSUMPTION 50 TO 60 MILES PER GALLON.
Complete with Windscreen & Hood, Electric Lighting Set & Full Kit of Tools, Etc.
Price £250 plus 5%, provisional.
C. E. RICHARDSON & Co. Ltd.,
AIZLEWOOD ROAD SHEFFIELD
Telephone: 36 SHARROW Telegrams: "FINBAT" SHEFFIELD
— Authorised Agents —

CHAPTER SIX

Sheffield tragedies

Steel City has endured loss on a massive scale countless times over the years. Memory of the recent Hillsborough Disaster will be with us for generations, other events such as the hundreds killed and injured in the Sheffield Blitz (often referred to as 'the forgotten Blitz') deserve more permanent commemoration.

Sheffield Flood of 1864

Became known as the biggest tragedy of its kind in Victorian England. Today little more than a commemorative stone buried in the undergrowth marks the devastating result of seven hundred million gallons of water pouring down from the Bradfield area of Sheffield right through the city centre, destroying virtually everything in its horrifying path.

The event occurred on a very stormy day – Friday, March 11, 1864. William Horsfield, a workman employed by the Water Company responsible for the Bradfield Reservoir (or Dale Dyke Dam as it was generally called) spotted a crack stretching some fifty yards about 5.30pm. He wasn't overly concerned and only mentioned it in passing to a farmer as he thought it was probably earlier frost damage and the dam wasn't in any danger.

It played on the farmer's mind; he visited the scene around 7pm and, duly alarmed, informed one of the water company's over lookers, Mr Swinden.

He arrived with a number of colleagues who were horrified to see the crack had widened but hardly able to communicate because of the wild storm and darkness.

They truly believed their valiant attempts to prevent further damage to the reservoir embankment by opening sluice pipes, to draw off the pressure of the water, had won the day and most of them had returned home.

Within minutes the unthinkable happened and the might of the water tore through an opening of nearly thirty feet. A few seconds later the entire embankment collapsed and with an unholy roar, one hundred and fourteen million cubic feet of water tore down the valley whose occupants were totally oblivious to the wall of death and destruction that was heading in the direction of Sheffield.

In short, 270 people were drowned in the tragedy, 798 homes were completely destroyed and nearly 5,000 houses were flooded.

The following is a return showing the number of buildings and houses destroyed or injured by the Bursting of the Bradfield Reservoir on the 12th of March 1864:

	Manufactories, Tilts, &c.			Rolling Grinding, Corn, and other Mills.			Workshops, Warehouses, Store Rooms, &c.			Draprs' Grocrs' and other Sale Shops.			Dwelling Houses.			Malt Houses, Breweries, Public and Beer-Houses.			Buildings not otherwise described.			Yards of Fence walling.
	Totally Destroyed.	Partially do.	Flooded only.	Totally Destroyed.	Partially do.	Flooded only.	Totally Destroyed.	Partially do.	Flooded only.	Totally Destroyed.	Partially do.	Flooded only.	Totally Destroyed.	Partially do.	Flooded only.	Totally Destroyed.	Partially do.	Flooded only.	Totally Destroyed.	Partially do.	Flooded only.	Totally Destroyed.
From the Dam to Malin Bridge	9	4					2			1			12	11	8							
Holm lane				1			9			1			3	7	23	1			2			440
Hillsbro'											3		1	1			2		4			
Hill Bridge				1	1								4	20		1						
Owlerton		2			6		3	3			3		1	39	164		2	5	9	5		454
Penistone Road		1	1									5			50			7			2	
Hill Foot						1			4		1	14		6	134			6	2	1		20
Philadelphia	2				4						1		3	19	68			4	4			1000
Bacon Island		1											3	19					5			
Rutland Road														7	21							
Cornish Place			3						1						11		1		1		1	
Cornish street									3			3			11							
Artisan street															28							
Dixon street									4			3			39							
Shalesmoor		1	1						2			86			14			4				
Dun street								2	7			1		1	57			3				
Dun lane															25							
Dun Fields															61			2				
Acorn street															43			1			2	
Ebenezer square															21							50
Ebenezer street															24							
Ward street									1						16						1	
Bowling Green-st			1												32			1				
Gibraltar street									6			47			28			5			1	
Ball street															24			1	1			
Long Croft			1						6						58							
Green lane		1	4						1			20			54			4				20
Kelham Island		2			1									4								190
Alma street						2						8			14			4				
Cotton Mill Walk									1						52							
Kelham street									2						29						1	
Russell street			2			1			9			8			45			4				
Bower Spring						1						7			23			3			2	
Cotton Mill Row			1						1						16						2	
Water street															17							
Spring street			3						8			1		1	40			4				
Corporation street						2			2			16			6			2			2	

	Manufactories, Tilts, &c.			Rolling Grinding, Corn, and other Mills.			Workshops, Warehouses, Store Rooms, &c.			Drapers' Grocers' and other Sale Shops.			Dwelling Houses.			Malt Houses, Breweries, Public and Beer-Houses.			Buildings not otherwise described.			Yards of Fence walling.
	Totally Destroyed.	Partially do.	Flooded only.	Totally Destroyed.	Partially do.	Flooded only.	Totally Destroyed.	Partially do.	Flooded only.	Totally Destroyed.	Partially do.	Flooded only.	Totally Destroyed.	Partially do.	Flooded only.	Totally Destroyed.	Partially do.	Flooded only.	Totally Destroyed.	Partially do.	Flooded only.	Totally Destroyed.
Bridge street			8			1						15		2	44			14			3	
Mill lane															12							
Pear street															10							
Steam street															6							
Plum street									2						9							
Love lane															15							
Cross Love street															18							
Love street			2			2			4						14			1			1	
Water lane																		2				
Waingate												3										
Millsands		1	2			2									53			1	4			80
Killing Shambles															1						1	
Old Park Wood				2	2									4					4			
Farfield					1			1					1	4	9		1		2			230
Neepsend lane	1	1								1	3		5	62	179		2	4	8			610
Lancaster street											1			2	5		1		1			50
Percy street								1					6	14	58		1					10
Ball street North		2									1			7	16			1				30
Mowbray street		3	5		1		1	1							70			3		2		54
Harvest lane									10			16		33	192		2	3				67
Baker's Row do.												1		1	23							
Duke street do.															28							
Orchard street do.									4			6		87	271		2	4		2	6	
Bridgehouses												14		5	32		2	2	3	1		
Nursery street		1	3		1				6			6		11	31		3	4	1		6	402
Nursery lane									4					1	32							
Spital Fields			1						7						7						6	
Johnson street			1			1						6			74			2				10
Johnson lane			1											1	23						1	6
Stanley street			1						7			11			61			2			3	56
Stanley lane									2			1			13						1	
Joiner street															29			1				
Joiner lane			3											1	24							
Andrew street			1												62			1				
Andrew lane									2						10							
Walker street			2												33			1			1	
School lane									2													
Gun lane									1						2							
Wicker		1	4			2	2	3	6		2	94		1	20		2	12	1			108
Wicker lane		1	3						2					3	37							
Willey street		1							4						38							
Blonk street			3						3			3			9		1		1			
Effingham street															14			1				
Saville street			5			3			3			4			64			6			21	174
Saville street east			6									4			94			6				
Sutherland street			2									4			60			4				
Greystock street		1										3			166			3				

	Manufactories, Tilts, &c.			Rolling Grinding, Corn, and other Mills.			Workshops, Warehouses, Store Rooms, &c.			Draprs' Grocrs' and other Sale Shops.			Dwelling Houses.			Malt Houses, Breweries, Public and Beer-Houses.			Buildings not otherwise described.			Yards of Fence walling.
	Totally Destroyed.	Partially do.	Flooded only.	Totally Destroyed.	Partially do.	Flooded only.	Totally Destroyed.	Partially do.	Flooded only.	Totally Destroyed.	Partially do.	Flooded only.	Totally Destroyed.	Partially do.	Flooded only.	Totally Destroyed.	Partially do.	Flooded only.	Totally Destroyed.	Partially do.	Flooded only.	Totally Destroyed.
Corby street									3			6			114			3				..
Princess street									1			6			173			3				..
Feresfield street												1			19							..
Noroy street												1			24							..
Windsor street															10							..
Royds' Mill street						1						4			2			1				..
Lovell street															31							..
Blackmore street												1			31			1				..
Tinsley road			4						4			15			150			8			3	..
Washford street			2												..							30
Slittingmill Farm															3						4	20
Brightside lane			3									3			43			2				20
Newhall			1											2	169			5				80
Brightside		1										4			91			1				267
Blackburn Tilt						3									2							..
TOTAL	12	25	80	4	17	22	17	11	135	3	15	451	39	376	4096	2	22	162	53	11	71	4478

There were also eleven churches, chapels, or schools flooded. Three tanneries and skin yards were partially destroyed. There were fifteen bridges totally destroyed and five partially destroyed.

Sheffield City Battalion

When war was declared on Germany on August 4, 1914, there was excitement all over town.

The city didn't have to try very hard to find willing volunteers to enlist in the Sheffield City Battalion at the Corn Exchange the following month.

Nearly 1,000 men signed up within two days. The heady atmosphere and overbearing confidence in the success of their forthcoming mission was captured on the placards of the time: 'To Berlin – Via [the] Corn Exchange' they rang out.

The recruits came from all walks of life: business men, stockbrokers, engineers, chemists, metallurgical experts, university and public school men, medical students, journalists, schoolmasters, craftsmen, shop assistants, secretaries and more.

Early drill took place at Bramall Lane football ground before they set up camp at Redmires on the outskirts of the city.

On July 1, 1916, Sheffield City Battalion played a lead part in one of the biggest military disasters in British history – the Battle of the Somme.

Five days of intense allied shelling of the German front was meant to have neutralised it. Some British soldiers were that cocksure of themselves they even took a football to kick about on the way.

Within minutes of them going over the top it was if the whole group had been wiped off the face of the earth by merciless German machine gun fire. 513 officers and men were either killed, wounded or missing – a further 75 slightly wounded.

John Harris, author of 'Covenant With Death', a book based on the story of the Sheffield City Battalion, describes their tragic life in three poignant sentences:

"Two years in the making. Ten minutes in the destroying. That was our history."

The Zeppelin Raid

It was just before 10pm one night in September 1916 when people living beyond the city's southern boundaries first spotted the huge airship cruising menacingly towards Sheffield.

Only a few months earlier it had been unthinkable for a civilian population sited hundreds of miles away from a battlefront to be in any danger whatsoever.

Sheffield learned a tragic lesson in the importance of air raid planning and readiness that night. The vast ship arrived almost unnoticed by the local anti-aircraft defence officers who were busy lording it up at a social function taking place at Leopold Street's Grand Hotel.

The defences were described as a "fiasco" and "shambolic" in the aftermath of the attack on the evening of September 25/26, 1916, that left 28 people killed and many more injured.

The Zeppelin began circling clockwise over the city to help get its bearings before dropping wave after wave of incendiaries and high explosives over the suburbs of Pitsmoor and Attercliffe.

Sheffield Daily Independent reported the aftermath in graphic detail at the time.

"The first case taken was that of a woman aged 36 years, wife of a labourer. Her husband said he hurried to the attic to fetch his children and take them into the cellar, and shouted to his wife to follow. As he reached the cellar there was an explosion. His wife exclaimed, "Oh Bill my leg's off". She died three hours afterwards.

"An elderly married woman got out of bed when the first bomb dropped and was passing across the room to get her child when a bomb struck her in the back, tearing it open. Her body was nearly severed at the trunk. She died in hospital."

Sheffield Blitz

Autumn 1940 was one of the most foreboding periods in Sheffield's history.

Hitler's Germany seemed unstoppable and a full-scale UK invasion seemed inevitable.

France had fallen and the Nazis were less than 25 miles from the South coast of England.

Sheffield's position as a key part of the country's war effort, via its munitions production, always made it key target but, despite all this, the city was gearing up to try and celebrate Christmas 1940.

It was Thursday, December 12. Resplendent city centre shopping institutions like Atkinsons, Cockaynes, Walshs, Redgates, C&A Modes and Marks & Spencer were decked out in festive finery despite the continued air of menace.

By early evening the city's bars, cinemas and theatres were packed to the rafters as Sheffielders put thoughts of the war behind them and decided to start to celebrate Christmas in earnest.

Within hours great swathes of the city centre had been utterly destroyed; hundreds were dead and dying and bombs had been dropped across the entire city, killing indiscriminately.

Scores of Sheffield's most famous shops had been flattened alongside famous old public houses like the King's Head, the Angel, the Westminster, the Royal Oak, the Bodega, the Devonshire Arms, the Shades Vaults and the Three Horse Shoes that were lost.

The bombers returned three nights later, leaving over 2,000 citizens killed or injured and 40,000 homeless.

Walk the streets of Sheffield in the 21st century and little evidence remains of those two horrific nights in December 1940 and the months it took to rebuild the city's shattered infrastructure.

Many now, sadly, refer to Sheffield as 'the forgotten Blitz'.

The Hillsborough Disaster

The darkest day in English football took place on the afternoon of April 15, 1989, at Hillsborough, home of Sheffield Wednesday. The Hillsborough Disaster traumatised an entire nation as a human crush resulted in the deaths of 96 Liverpool fans with 766 injured.

The FA Cup semi-final between Liverpool and Nottingham Forest was abandoned after six minutes at the realisation of the unfolding tragedy.

The inquiry into the disaster, the Taylor Report, blamed failure of police control, and resulted in the conversion of many football stadiums in the United Kingdom to all-seater and the removal of barriers at the front of stands.

THE SHEFFIELD CLUB.

The Sheffield Club that used to
sit on Norfolk Street

CHAPTER SEVEN

Sheffield's music heritage trail

"Outside of the capital, Sheffield has consistently produced more quality rock acts since the '60s than any other metropolis bar Manchester." Tim Perry, Rock & Roll Traveller to Great Britain and Ireland.

Site of the Crazy Daizy:

Former High Street underground disco that became internationally renowned as the place where Human League front man Philip Oakey first clapped eyes on schoolgirls Susan Sulley and Joanne Catherall.

By early 1981 they were a key part of the new–look band that became megastars the world over and continue to record and perform to this day.

Site of The Limit:

Legendary Sheffield venue that played host to the UK live debut of the B-52s and saw 13 people turn up to watch some young guns from Ireland by the name of U2 when no one else was interested in booking them.

The Limit was the venue for the one and only time city rock act Def Leppard supported the Human League. The club also promoted seminal gigs for other local outfits including Vice Versa (who went on to become ABC), Cabaret Voltaire and Clock DVA.

The Limit shut in 1991 after 13 years of live mayhem and club nights.

Black Swan (now The Boardwalk), Snig Hill:

The venue that hosted the live debut of The Clash on Sunday, July 4, 1976. Supporting the Sex Pistols, they were absolutely awful by all accounts.

Wapentake Bar (now The Casbah), Cambridge Street:

Subterranean rock bar that staged one of the first live outings of Def Leppard. They returned in 1995 with the eyes of the world's music press on them and performed an acoustic set in front of 300 VIP guests. They were paid £15 for their first performance in the late seventies. 17 years later they waived their fee.

The gig was part of Sheffield's 'Def Leppard Day' which saw the band unveil plaques at Crookes Working Men's Club and Don Valley Stadium.

Jarvis Cocker accident site:

Pulp front man Jarvis Cocker's appearance in a wheelchair in the late '80s caused quite a stir amongst the band's growing army of fans.

Whilst some thought it a quirky stage prop – the tale behind it was rather more bizarre.

The tale centres around a window somewhere above The Private Shop that resides at 68 Division Street . The gangly gent was doing his utmost to impress a girl and ended up falling out the window and breaking his legs. We never found out if he got the girl or not.

National Centre for Popular Music (now Hallam Union Building of Sheffield (HUBs)):

Take a stroll on Paternoster Row and gaze in wonderment at what might have been...

Club 60, Shalesmoor:

Terry Thornton opened the original venue in 1960 which hosted gigs by future Sheffield stars Jimmy Crawford (the city's first chart star), Dave Berry and Frank White. Terry Thornton went on to open the Esquire.

Esquire, Leadmill Road:

The upstairs of what is now The Leadmill used to be home to the Esquire in the sixties. From home-grown Joe Cocker (then Vance Arnold and the Avengers) to a veritable who's who of rock of the era including The Kinks and The Small Faces. The Leadmill carry on the live band tradition to this day and have been doing so for the past 30 years.

The Fiesta (now the Odeon Cinema), Arundel Gate:

Opened in the summer of 1970, the Fiesta was as near the city ever got to Las Vegas. The legendary cabaret club entertained the Sheffield crowds with the likes of Stevie Wonder, The Jacksons and region's own Tony Christie. T-Rex wasn't so impressed. Front man Marc Bolan turned up to play, decided it wasn't his type of venue and went home again. It was left to comedian Jack Diamond to pick up the pieces (who apparently went down quite well after an, understandably, shaky start).

Sheffield Lyceum:

Now back to its original format as a resplendent Victorian theatre, the venue spent a couple of years in the early eighties as a live music venue. Staged a legendary two night homecoming for Human League and Sheffield return visits for two acts that played seminal shows in Sheffield in their infancy – The Clash and U2.

King Mojo:

The venue that truly put Peter Sringfellow on the sixties map. No alcohol, but every band of note from the era spanning Hendrix to Pink Floyd.

Sheffield City Hall, Barker's Pool:

Opening in 1932, the building got the shock of its life when rock'n'roll first entered in the sixties with the likes of The Beatles. But it moved with the times and became a heavy metal stronghold in the 1980s and still thrives to this day

CHAPTER EIGHT

Sheffield on the silver screen

The city has had no shortage of appearances on the TV and cinema screens down the years. Here's a few notable highlights...

This Is England '86 (2010) – The TV spin-off by celebrated film maker Shane Meadows was filmed in the down-at-heel Gleadless Valley.

Four Lions (2010) – Christopher Morris-directed story of a group of British jihadists who push their abstract dreams of glory to the breaking point. Much of the London-based climax is actually set just behind Debenhams, off The Moor, in Sheffield.

Whatever Happened to Harold Smith? (1999) – once tipped as the next Full Monty but didn't have the staying power. A love story set in 1970s Sheffield starring Tom Courtenay, Lulu, Stephen Fry and others.

The Full Monty (1997) – One of the highest grossing comedy films of all time which made Sheffield famous around the globe. Some thought it gave the wrong impression of the city; most thought our wit and tenacity shone through like never before. The plot centres around a bunch of unemployed steelworkers who turn to striptease to make ends meet.

When Saturday Comes (1996) – Sean Bean stars in the story of a factory worker who gets scouted, firstly by non-league side Hallam F.C. and then later by Sheffield United Football Club.

Tales From A Hard City (1995) - Alex Usborne and Kim Flitcroft's gritty drama/documentary that took on a cult status in later years. The plot revolves around four dreamers (the dirty dancer, the hustler, the thief and the media mogul) looking for a break in Sheffield.

Hitman & Her (1988-1992) – The car crash of a late night TV show starring Pete Waterman and Michaela Strachan was regularly filmed at Sheffield's Roxy venue.

Threads (1984)– Apocalyptic vision of what would happen to Sheffield in the wake of a nuclear attack. The British TV drama was written by Barry Hines and released at the height of the Cold War. Does little to up the mood.

Looks And Smiles (1981) – Ken Loach directed adaptation of the Barry Hines book of the same name. Some of the film was shot in Sheffield's legendary Limit club. Set against the foreboding backdrop of Thatcher's Britain.

City On The Move (1972) – Sheffield promotional film that inadvertently became a global success years later thanks to part of it being included to front The Full Monty. Made by Jim and Marie-Luise Coulthard, the film was released on DVD as The Reel Monty.

The Life Of Charles Peace (1905) – Sheffield's master criminal was the subject of a very early melodrama directed by William Haggar.

VICTORIA PARK HOTEL,

(OPPOSITE THE BOTANICAL GARDENS,)

Commercial & Family Boarding House,

SHEFFIELD.

JOHN LAW, PROPRIETOR.

WINES, &c., OF THE PUREST AND BEST QUALITY.

BOWLING GREEN & AMERICAN BOWLING ALLEY.

DINNER & TEA PARTIES will find excellent accommodation.

JOHN LAW,

LANDSCAPE GARDENER,

VICTORIA PARK, SHEFFIELD.

Plans and Estimates furnished for Villa Residences or Greenhouses.

OMNIBUSES pass hourly to and from the Station.

FEARLESS.

KOH-I-NOOR

ESTABLISHED 1828.

SOHO

"HOBSONS CHOICE."

TOUGH AND STRONG ALBION.

HOBSON, HOUGHTON & Co. LTD.

Don Steel Works, SHEFFIELD

ENGLAND

(Incorporating GEO. FISHER & Co. and GREGORY & BRAMALL)

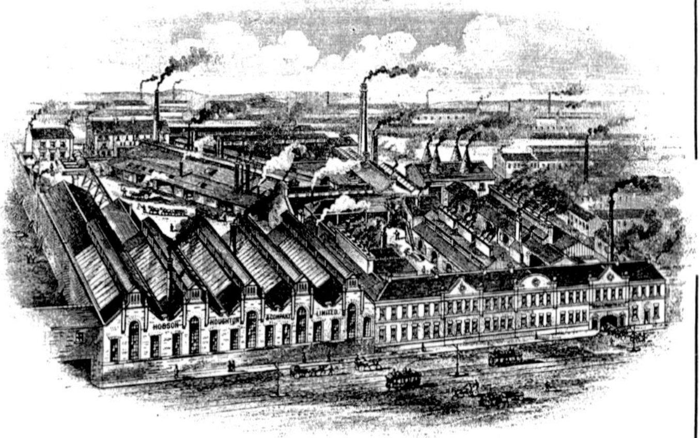

MANUFACTURERS OF

HIGH-SPEED STEELS in three grades: "FEARLESS," "ALBION SPECIAL," and "ALBION"; SELF-HARDENING STEEL; NICKEL-CHROME, VANADIUM, and other ALLOY STEELS for Aircraft, Motor Car, and other purposes; HIGH QUALITY CRUCIBLE STEELS for all purposes; NEEDLE WIRE for Sewing Machine Needles, HOSIERY and LATCH NEEDLES; WIRE-DRAWERS' PLATES; MINING STEELS in all sections; TWIST DRILLS; FILES and RASPS (Sole Makers of the celebrated "FISHER" and "FEARLESS" BRANDS).

UNITED STATES BRANCH:
WAREHOUSE—
83, BEEKMAN STREET,
NEW YORK

LONDON OFFICE:
63, QUEEN VICTORIA STREET, E.C. 4

CHAPTER NINE

Sheffield in numbers

Total population for city and metropolitan borough in 2011: 534,500.

Total population in 1086: 150-200

" " in 1736: 9,695

" " in 1821: 65, 375

" " in 1861: 185, 172

" " in 1911: 455, 817.

Sheffield's student population in 2011: 54,000.

Cost of the city's Supertram network: £240 million.

Length of Supertram network: 29 kilometres.

Population made homeless in the Sheffield Blitz: 40,000.

Sheffield is built on seven hills and is near the confluence of five rivers.

It is England's fourth largest city and it is estimated to have two million trees within its boundaries.

Sheffield invested £200m in new sporting facilities for the World Student Games in 1991.

Sheffield has 78 public parks.

80% of vehicles travelling to and from Sheffield city centre are cars, 11% are light goods vehicles and 3.5% are buses.

36% of Sheffield households don't have a car/van, compared with a figure of 27% nationally.

The rise and (rapid) fall of the Sheffield car industry

Though its efforts have been largely forgotten, Sheffield did try its hand in the burgeoning motor industry in the early part of the last century.

It wasn't surprising considering the city's position as a world epicentre of steel production.

The most notable name will always be the 'Sheffield Simplex' – luxury cars that were sold to princes, czars and other global nobility. The first models were the LA1 and LA2.

They definitely ranked alongside the Rolls Royce and were the city's longest produced cars. The Tinsley-based operation even had its own showroom in London.

The depression and other factors of the inter-war years sadly saw off Sheffield's valiant attempts in the trade. All that remains these days are the odd museum piece (you should be able to see a splendid Simplex at the city's Kelham Island Museum)

JOHN WALSH, Ltd.,

Complete Outfitters.

WHETHER YOU ARE

Walking or Cycling

And you wish to enjoy to the full, the charm of complete freedom and comfort – be careful to select the right Clothing and Footwear . . . .

Comfortable Footwear

Is perhaps the most important item of all—in fact we make it a Specialite. You will find we stock thoroughly well seasoned Boots, well cut and well made, suitable for all kinds of out-door wear The Prices throughout are very moderate . . . .

Serviceable Suits

Ready to wear in all the best Tweeds, Etc. We always stock a large selection of Gent.'s and Boys' Suits—really useful Out-door Garments that will stand any kind of weather—in the latest correct styles, cut to perfection, and just ready to put on. Cycling suits receive special attention. . . . .

Suitable Underwear

In all the best makes. Gent.'s Tunic Shirts, Soft Oxford and Print Shirts, Cellular Shirts, Etc. We would especially recommend a trial of the Cellular Underwear, it is unequalled for health and comfort. Hats, Caps, Gloves, and Hosiery at all prices, in all the Newest makes.

RELIABLE GOODS AT THE LOWEST PRICES.

WE CATER ESPECIALLY FOR

THE TOURIST,
THE ATHLETE, and
THE CYCLIST.

44 to 64, High Street,

SHEFFIELD.

CHAPTER TEN

Where to go out in 1879

If you were a monied up industrialist in Victorian Sheffield there was opportunity a plenty for a cultured night on the town. You could laud it up with fellow members at the Sheffield Club or impress your friends and hire out The Cutlers' Hall. Here's how things were described back then:

THE CUTLERS' HALL, in Church-street, the splendid rooms of which are occasionally used for balls, dinners, and meetings of a more or less public character. For township and district meetings, &c., the various Vestry Halls are let on easy terms.

THE ALBERT HALL, designed for musical entertainments and large public meetings, was opened on the 14th December, 1873, and is the property of a Joint Stock Company. It is centrally situated – but on a much too crowded site – at the junction of Barker's-pool and Burgess-street. The building is of red brick, relieved by granite pillars and carved stone cornice and tracings but is remarkable rather for hugeness of appearance than for external beauty. The large concert room is 60 feet wide and 125 feet long. The organ, and an orchestra – arranged to hold 168 chorus singers, with band and soloists – occupy one end. The saloon is the full width of the room and 103 feet long; and there is a two-tier balcony at the west end, and a gallery above it. The saloon will seat 1,000 auditors, the balcony and stalls 700, and the gallery 500, - seats for a total of 2,200 persons, exclusive of the orchestra. The concert room is 50 feet high, the ceiling being hexagonal in shape, with a view to acoustic excellence, which has been most fully attained. Not the least attraction of the Albert Hall, in a musical sense, is the magnificent organ, erected by the celebrated French builder Mons. Cavaille Coll, at a cost of £5,000.

The case – from a design by Mons. Semil, a Parisian architect of eminence in this class of work – is of oak and Canadian pine. The organ is of immense size, having 74 stops and 4,064 pipes, is constructed with all the latest pneumatic and other improvements, and is in every respect admirably made. The perfection of its mechanism has excited the admiration of the English builders who have examined it. Not less marvellous is the instrument in respect of its immense power, the variety and exquisite clearness of its tones, and the grandeur of its combinations, which musical men agree in saying have never been equalled and probably never surpassed. It is unquestionably one of the best organs in the country.

MUSIC HALL, in Surrey-street, was erected in 1823, and belongs, like the Albert Hall, to a company of Proprietors. The lower rooms are occupied by the Sheffield Library. Previous to the opening of the Albert Hall the large upper rooms were chiefly used for concerts, but are now occupied as a High School for Girls.

TEMPERANCE HALLS – The Sheffield Temperance Society have a Hall in Townhead-street, which was built in 1855-66, at a cost of about £2,500. The principal room is 81 feet long by 51 feet wide, and having a gallery at the end, will accommodate nearly 2,000 people. The Hall is let for lectures, political, trade, and other meetings and entertainments.

FREEMASONS' HALL – The Freemasons have a Hall at the corner of Surrey-street and Eyre-street, which though not particularly handsome externally, is a building of which they have good reason to be proud. The Hall is the property of a Limited Liability Company, the shares in which are held exclusively by the several lodges and by individual members of the craft. The Freemasons purchased, in 1860, the building previously occupied by the Sheffield and Hallamshire Savings Bank, and some years later they also bought the adjoining house in Surrey-street. The new Hall was built upon the site of the old Savings Bank in 1876, and comprises a banqueting room on the ground floor and lodge room over it. The rooms are lofty, and are each 51 feet long and

26 feet wide. They are well built of stone, handsomely fitted and furnished, effectively warmed by hot water, and ventilated on the system recently patented by Mr. Tobin. The lodge room, which is particularly handsome, has an arched roof springing from the cornice, and ornamented with moulded ribs, panels, and carved bosses, the walls being relieved by columns with foliated capitals springing from ornamental corbels. The lodge and banqueting rooms are approached by broad passages from the adjoining building, which comprises steward's room, kitchens, and lavatory on the ground floor, cloak and robing rooms on the first floor, and rooms for a resident hall-keeper on the second floor, and rooms for a resident hall-keeper on the second floor.

THE ARTILLERY DRILL HALL, in course of erection, in Clough-road, for the use of the Artillery Volunteers, and described elsewhere, will be a valuable addition to the large rooms available for public gatherings and entertainments.

THE SHEFFIELD CLUB is an institution for social purposes similar to the Clubs in London. It is supported by the elite of the town, and carried on with great spirit. The Club House in Norfolk-street, was opened in 1862; the style of the architecture being Palladian freely treated. In its erection, stateliness of appearance has been combined with the best internal arrangements. Every provision has been made for substantial comfort and for the amusements usual in such institutions. The cost of the building and fittings exceeded £7,000.

THE ATHENEUM, which was established in 1847, occupies commodious premises in George-street, which were purchased and remodelled in 1859 and further improved in 1873. The building belongs to the Company of Proprietors, and is let free of rent, the condition being that four £5 shares shall entitle the holder to membership in, and all the advantages of, the Athenaeum free of charge; and one share, to the same privileges on payment of a yearly subscription of £1. The subscription for non-shareholders is £1 10s., and for ladies 10s a year. The Athenaeum combines the advantages of a Club with the addition of a commodious and well supplied newsroom and extensive library. The newsroom and library are on the ground floor and also well furnished private rooms for the use of the lady members. On the second floor is a large dining and coffee room and a club-room. Dr. M. Martin de Bartolome is the president, and Mrs. Webster, librarian and secretary.

WORKING MEN'S CLUBS. – The movement for establishing Working Men's Clubs in Sheffield began in 1871. Ecclesall Club, adjoining South-street, Sheffield-moor, being opened in the early part of the year. Similar institutions were subsequently opened in other parts of the town. St. Peter's Club, held in the Old Council Hall, at the junction of Norfolk-street and Arundel-street, was opened in August 1872. It has dining and coffee room, billiard rooms, reading, smoke, and club rooms, all of which are largely resorted to. Concerts and other entertainments are occasionally given on winter evenings. Refreshments of all kinds are supplied at the working men's clubs as at the more expensive clubs of the wealthier classes. Among the more successful suburban clubs are St. George's, Westernbank, and Highfield Club, London-road. The dinner is a much less important feature than of St. Peter's, which has a crowded mid-day "ordinary", but members have the advantage of out-door recreation in the summer evenings. There are workmen's clubs at Attercliffe, Grimesthorpe, &c. Several of the clubs own the premises they occupy; they are fairly prosperous.

ESTABLISHED 1759.

Thomas Porter & Sons,

Dealers in High-class

Teas, Coffees

AND

GENERAL GROCERIES,

CHOICE DESSERT FRUITS,

Chocolates, Fondants, &c.

T. P. & S. Invite attention to their

Oriental Department

In which they have always on SHOW a Large and Varied Assortment of

Japanese and Chinese Vases, Bowls, Bronzes, Trays, Ivory Carvings, Screens, Gongs, &c., &c.,

SUITABLE FOR

BIRTHDAY and WEDDING PRESENTS.

7 & 9, KING ST., SHEFFIELD.

TELEPHONE 300.

CHAPTER ELEVEN

Seven wonders of Sheffield

Whilst we might lack our very own Hanging Gardens of Babylon we've still plenty we hold dear in our fine city. The following might not be set for World Heritage status any day soon but we'll be dining out on them for decades...

Tinsley Towers (wonders one and two) – Nobody could quite believe they'd gone. It was tantamount to our very own Princess Di moment with thousands turning out in the middle of the night to say their goodbyes. We'd have probably laid flowers if only EON had let us onto the site. The iconic towers had become a landmark for decades standing 250 feet tall by the side of Tinsley Viaduct. Despite campaigns to save them, they were demolished in August 2008.

Hole In The Road – This was another fantastic idea that fell out of favour and was left to go to total rack and ruin. When it opened in the autumn of 1967 it was the apple of everyone's eye and could do no wrong. The subterranean cluster of passageways, escalators, shops, seats and mesmerising fish tank. It became affectionately known as the 'Hole In The Road' and soon earned its rightful place in Sheffield folklore. Jarvis Cocker even cited it as an inspiration. By the eighties and early nineties it was becoming a 'no go area at night', the escalators never worked and the shops were shutting. In the mid 1990s it was filled in.

Coles Corner – Before mobile phones totally eradicated the need to make firm arrangements the entire city arranged to meet at this hallowed spot at the bottom of Fargate.

Coles Corner must have been that busy it's a miracle anyone found anyone. Richard Hawley brought it to national prominence with his album of the same name. Coles (now John Lewis) has long gone (it's opposite Sheffield City Hall) and these days the space is occupied by a rather faceless HSBC bank.

Park Hill Flats – There's no doubt the idea behind the 'streets in the sky' was genius. Things just didn't work out that well in practice. But they ain't going anywhere soon as they've been listed; so you might as well look on in awe and remember their halcyon days in the sixties. They were actually opened in 1961 by Roy Hattersley, then chair of housing at Sheffield City Council. One of its pubs, The Parkway Tavern, had the dubious honour of appearing on Sky One's 'Toughest Pubs in Britain' programme. It's hard to miss Park Hill Flats – they dominate the entire skyline behind the railway station.

Parson Cross Estate – Sadly, better known as the epicentre of anti-social behaviour these days, this sprawling estate provided dream homes for thousands of people coming out of slum housing in the 1940s and 1950s. One of the biggest estates of its type in the country, many of the houses were built by Italian POWs. It had its own cinema, pubs and more. Books are now being written on the joys of growing up there in years gone by.

Millhouses Park Lido – Sheffield was once home to the mother of all outdoor swimming pools. Millhouses Park Lido was a legend and the entire city used to flock there in the hot summers of the 1970s. Some blamed the climate for it falling it out of favour. We think we're just not as hardy as our elders. A speciality of the local Spartans swimming club was taking to the water in freezing cold weather in decades gone by. There's even a film of them taking a dip in the park in the 1930s. Today there's little more than a water play park for youngsters. A crying shame.

DAVY BROTHERS,

PARK IRON WORKS, SHEFFIELD,

ENGINEERS, MILLWRIGHTS & MACHINISTS,

IRON AND BRASS FOUNDERS,

MANUFACTURERS OF LOCOMOTIVE ENGINES AND OTHER RAILWAY PLANT,

IMPROVED VERTICAL AND HORIZONTAL ENGINES,

ON THE HIGH-PRESSURE, CONDENSING, AND COMPOUND PRINCIPLES.

PUMPING AND WINDING ENGINES, FOR COLLIERY & MINING PURPOSES.

LARGE LIFT AND PLUNGE PUMPS.

PORTABLE STEAM ENGINES,

FOR AGRICULTURAL AND OTHER PURPOSES.

Vertical Saw Frames and Circular Saw Frames &c. Punching and Shearing Machines, for Boiler Makers. Paring and Scrap Cutting Shears, and Boiler Makers' Tools of every description. Improved Steam Hammers, Single and Double Acting, and Small Steam Hammers for the Tilting of Steel and Light Smith Work. SUGAR MILLS of all Sizes. Sugar Kettles, Tanks, Bull Pumps, and Hand Pumps, and other Machinery for Sugar Estates. Patent Axles of every description.

DAVY BROTHERS having an extensive plant, are prepared to execute orders with the greatest promptitude and in the best manner possible, and particularly call the attention of the public to their Improved Portable Steam Engines.

Drawing and Specifications of all kinds of Engineering Work can be had on application.

SLACK'S Cream Toffee is sublime,
'Twill keep you smiling all the time.—*Cherridine.*

CANE SUGAR!
FINEST BUTTER!!
PUREST CREAM!!!

SLACK'S
CREAM
TOFFEE.

The IDEAL Sweetmeat.

Sale Enormous and . .
STILL INCREASING.

STEAM CONFECTIONERY WORKS:

45, SCOTLAND ST.,

SHEFFIELD.

Branches: 126, THE MOOR. 83, SCOTLAND ST.
And NORFOLK MARKET HALL.

But Ask for Slack's.
But Ask for Slack's.

CHAPTER TWELVE

Local legends

One of Sheffield City Council's most popular moves of recent years has been allowing the public to vote for high profile Sheffielders (both alive and dead) whose names should adorn brass plaques in the pavement to make up the city's own 'walk of fame'.

New names are added at regular intervals and they're sited opposite the front entrance to the town hall on Pinstone Street.

Names getting the green light to date are:

- Gordon Banks - England's World Cup winning goal-keeper
- Sean Bean – actor and preferred voiceover for a million and one TV ads
- Joe Cocker – Sheffield singing legend
- Sebastian Coe - Olympic medal winner and Chair of the London 2012 Organising Committee
- Derek Dooley –football legend who won the respect of both the kops of SUFC and SWFC
- Professor Barry Hancock – cancer treatment specialist
- Brendan Ingle - boxing trainer who led Nasim Hamid and others to glory

- Def Leppard – Sheffield's biggest global music export
- David Mellor - internationally renowned cutlery designer
- Michael Palin – former Python stalwart turned global traveller
- Helen Sharman - first British astronaut
- Joe Simpson – mountaineer and author
- Joe Scarborough – barge-living artist
- Michael Vaughan - one of the UK's most successful cricket captains
- Clinton Woods - world champion boxer.

CHAPTER THIRTEEN

Soon to be legends...

Examples of other notables (both alive and dead) who are from Sheffield or have strong links with the city who could be joining the pavement glitterati in future months and years if the public see fit...

- ABC (Martin Fry fronted eighties stars – formerly Vice Versa)
- Alastair Burnet (news reader)
- Arctic Monkeys – all conquering Sheffield band
- Arthur Baynes aka Stainless Stephen (music hall comedian)
- Bailey Brothers (miners turned MTV presenters and 'air guitar' pioneers)
- Barry Hines (author)
- Bobby Knutt (actor and comedian)
- Brian Glover (actor/wrestler)
- Bring Me The Horizon (21st century tattooed boys of ferocious metal music)
- Dave Berry (musician)

- Eddie Izzard (comedian)
- Graham Fellows (the comedian/actor behind John Shuttleworth/Jilted John and more)
- Heaven 17 (hit making eighties outfit that rose from the ashes of the Human League)
- Human League (legendary electro rockers)
- Iron Maiden's plane flying, swashbuckling (literally) front man Bruce Dickinson
- Kate Rusby (folk singer)
- Keith Barron (actor)
- Leslie Ash (actress)
- Linda Smith (comedian)
- Marti Caine (comedian)
- Matthew Bannister (broadcaster)
- Nick Park (animator and film director)
- Patrick McGoohan (actor)
- Paul Carrack (musician)
- Pete Gill – former Glitter Band/Saxon/Motorhead drummer
- Peter Stringfellow - flamboyant nightclub owner
- Pulp – indie rockers who spawned Jarvis Cocker
- Ray Ashcroft (musician/actor)

- Richard H. Kirk (musician)
- Richard Hawley (solo star/former Longpigs member)
- Róisín Murphy (musician, formerly lead singer of Moloko)
- Thomas Craig – actor
- Tony Capstick (comedian/actor/musician/broadcaster)

. . Of Interest to Tourists, Cyclists, Motorists, &c., &c. . .

PRIEST & ASHMORE,

Manufacturing Opticians,

Newton Works, Earl St., Moor,

SHEFFIELD.

We make a distinct speciality of high-class work in

FIELD & OPERA GLASSES.

PRISMATIC BINOCULARS.

BINOCULAR TELESCOPES.

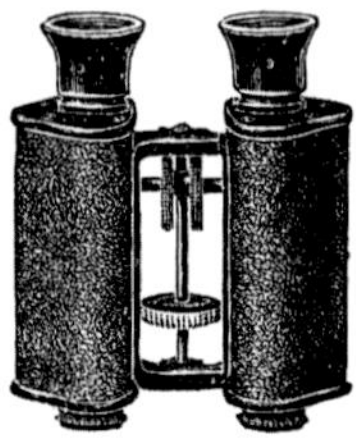

Fitted with finest hand-worked Lenses.

PERFECT ACHROMATISM. SPLENDID DEFINITION.

ACCURACY. DURABILITY.

CHAPTER FOURTEEN

Where to sleep and dine in Victorian Sheffield

If you arrived in the city in the late summer of 1862 you'd have just been in time to sample the delights of the newly opened Victoria Hotel and you'd hopefully leave just before the Sheffield Flood of 1864.

Pawson & Brailsford's Illustrated Guide to Sheffield And Neighbourhood said of it in 1862:

"This has been supplied by a number of shareholders, who have erected, at a cost of about £15,000, the Victoria Hotel, a spacious building adjoining the station of the Manchester, Sheffield, and Lincolnshire Railway... The hotel is one of the finest in the kingdom. It is five stories high and along with the ordinary range of lofty public rooms on the ground floor has billiard and smoke rooms, suites of private rooms, and upwards of fifty bedrooms. It is leased by Mr. George Meyer, of Manchester, who has expended near £10,000 in fittings and furnishing, and will be opened in July.

"There are other excellent inns in town. Such, for instance, are the Royal Hotel, at the corner of Waingate and Castle-folds; the Angel, in Angel-street; the King's Head, in Change-alley; the Commercial, Old Haymarket; the Black Swan, in Snig-hill; The George, Market-place; and others.

"A great convenience to persons residing in the suburbs and strangers visiting the town are the Commercial dining-rooms, the best of which are Mr. Eaton's in High-street; Mr. Bland's in the Haymarket; and Mr. Steer's, at the top of Dixon-lane."

Girls' Public Day School Company Limited,

IN CONNECTION WITH THE

NATIONAL UNION FOR IMPROVING THE EDUCATION OF WOMEN.

President of the Union:
HER ROYAL HIGHNESS PRINCESS LOUISE, MARCHIONESS OF LORNE.

President: THE EARL OF AIRLIE.

Chairman of the Council: W. H. STONE, Esq.

SHEFFIELD HIGH SCHOOL,

SURREY STREET, SHEFFIELD.

HEAD MISTRESS - MRS. WOODHOUSE.

THE AIM OF THE COMPANY

Is, by the employment of an ample staff of competent Teachers and the use of the best methods of instruction, to ensure for Girls an education adapted to their requirements, but as sound and thorough as that which Boys now receive in Grammar Schools of the highest class.

THE SCHOOL COURSE

Includes Religious Instruction, Reading, Writing, Arithmetic and Mathematics, Book-keeping, English Grammar, Composition and Literature, History, Geography, French, German, Latin, the Elements of Physical Science, Social Economy, Drawing, Class Singing and Harmony, Gymnastic Exercises and Needlework, or such of the above or other Subjects as the Council, with due regard to particular circumstances, may determine.

THE SCHOOL YEAR

Is divided into Three Terms, each of about Thirteen Weeks.

THE HOURS OF ATTENDANCE

Are from 9.30 to 1.30 every day but Saturday (which is a whole holiday).
Regular and punctual attendance is required.
Lessons in Music, and Special Drawing Lessons are given in the Afternoon.
The Pupils can attend between 2.30 and 4, to be assisted by the Teachers to prepare their lessons.

VACATIONS.

About Three days at Easter, and Eight days a fortnight later; about Seven weeks at Midsummer; and about Four weeks at Christmas. There is a whole holiday in the middle of each Term.

FEES (PAYABLE IN ADVANCE).

Entrance Fee—One Guinea.

TERM FEES.

For Pupils under Ten Years of Age	THREE GUINEAS a Term.
For the above Pupils remaining after Ten, and for Pupils entering the School between Ten and Thirteen Years of Age	FOUR GUINEAS a Term during the whole of their stay in the School.
For Pupils entering the School above Thirteen Years of Age	FIVE GUINEAS a Term during the whole of their stay in the School.

School Stationery (not including Drawing Materials) Five Shillings a Term.

Prospectuses and Forms, to be filled up before admission, may be obtained at the School, or from the Secretary of the Company, 112, Brompton road, London, S.W.

A. McDOWALL, B.A., B.Sc., SECRETARY.

CHAPTER FIFTEEN

Iconic department stores

Redgates:

Sheffield's finest ever toy store originally started life as far back as 1857 as an outlet for sewing machines and fur. Its shop on The Moor was completely flattened in the Sheffield Blitz and they re-located to Ecclesall Road. The latter years of Redgates were spent in their multi-level Furnival Gate store. It shut in 1988.

Any self respecting Sheffielder over thirty will remember wandering open-mouthed among three floors of Lego, dolls houses, Subbuteo, Meccano, bikes, buggies, goal posts, Spiderman outfits, Matchbox cars, railway sets, wooden horses and board games, with staff on hand to demonstrate.

The whole thing was so appealing a police officer called to investigate a shop-lifting once reprimanded the management.

He told them it was their own fault for making the store so attractive to children that they could hardly be blamed for snatching something!

Atkinsons:

Sheffield's only surviving independent department store and a true survivor, having fought everything from pedestrianisation of The Moor (where it stands) to Goring's Luftwaffe (who ensured it didn't stand, at least not on its Moor site, for nearly two decades).

Walsh's:

A true tour de force of Sheffield retail of days gone by. Originally started on the morning of 19 June 1875, when John Walsh opened a small baby linen and ladies' outfitting shop. It grew into a department store of formidable proportions with daily orchestra ensembles. Wiped off the face of the earth in the Sheffield Blitz but was rebuilt and came back.

Cockaynes:

Founded in 1829 by two brothers on Angel Street, this was another massive home-grown retail institution of awe-inspiring proportions. It sold out to Schofields in later years, who were only too happy to uphold its principles of quality and good service together with an a la carte restaurant and more.

John Banners:

The centre of Sheffield's East End in its heyday, John Banners department store was home to the first escalator in the city. Unlike the majority of the city centre department store architecture that was levelled in December 1940, the building still stands proud despite the tacky porn–charged suburban blight that surrounds it.

John Walsh Ltd
SUMMER
SALE
Commences Sat. July 16 1921
Doors Open 10am for first 3 mornings
HIGH STREET, SHEFFIELD

Saucy Sheffield

Henderson's Relish is practically mother's milk in Steel City, a sauce so common place that even some hairdressers sell it.

Henderson's is a similar consistency to Lea and Perrins, but with the flavour of a sharper, sweet brown sauce. Sold almost exclusively in Sheffield and the surrounding area, it has been made in the city since 1889. It is used as a relish on virtually everything and virtually indispensable both on local pies and everything else.

EXCHANGE DRAPERY ESTABLISHMENT

R. & G. GRAY & CO.

RESPECTFULLY CALL ATTENTION TO THIER

CHOICE AND FIRST-CLASS STOCK OF

FOREIGN & BRITISH SILKS

AND SILK VELVETS,

Mantles in all the New Materials and latest Shapes,

FOREIGN & PAISLEY SHAWLS,

FURS OF EVERY DESCRIPTION,

Paris and London Millinery Bonnets,

PLAIN & FANCY STRAW BONNETS & HATS,

FRENCH & ENGLISH FLOWERS, FEATHERS, &c., &c.,

LACES, RIBBONS, AND FANCY GOODS,

HOSE, GLOVES, AND TRIMMINGS,

BERLIN WOOL.

EVERY ARTICLE MARKED IN PLAIN FIGURES.

VICTORIA BUILDINGS, FARGATE,

SHEFFIELD.

VICTORIA BUILDINGS, FARGATE, SHEFFIELD.

LACE, TULLE, AND TARLATAN

BALL & EVENING ROBES,

FRENCH & NORWICH FANCY DRESSES,

FRENCH MERINOES, COBOURGS, &c.,

TABLE LINEN & SHEETINGS,

BLANKETS, QUILTS,

CRUMB CLOTHS, &c.

German, Swiss & Nottingham Curtains,

WOOLLEN CLOTHS,

BABY LINEN & LADIES' UNDERCLOTHING,

SEWED MUSLIN GOODS, HABERDASHERY, &c.,

FAMILY MOURNING OF EVERY DESCRIPTION.

EVERY ARTICLE MARKED IN PLAIN FIGURES.

R. & G. GRAY & Co.,

EXCHANGE DRAPERY ESTABLISHMENT,

FARGATE, SHEFFIELD.

CHAPTER SIXTEEN

Sheffield in the Domesday Book

The Domesday Book of 1086 contains the earliest known reference to the districts around Sheffield as the manor of "Hallun" (or Hallam). This manor retained its Saxon lord, Waltheof, for some years after the Norman Conquest. The Domesday Book was ordered by William the Conqueror so that the value of the townships and manors of England could be assessed. The entries in the Domesday Book are written in a Latin shorthand; the extract for our area begins:

TERRA ROGERII DE BVSLI

M. hi Hallvn, cu XVI bereuvitis sunt. XXIX. carucate trae

Ad gld. Ibi hb Walleff com aula...

Translated it reads:

LANDS OF ROGER DE BUSLI

In Hallam, one manor with its sixteen hamlets, there are twenty-nine carucates [~14 km^2] to be taxed. There Earl Waltheof had an "Aula" [hall or court]. There may have been about twenty ploughs. This land Roger de Busli holds of the Countess Judith. He has himself there two carucates [~1 km^2] and thirty-three villeins hold twelve carucates and a half [~6 km^2]. There are eight acres [32,000 m^2] of meadow, and a pasturable wood, *four leuvae in length and four in breadth [~10 km^2]. The whole manor is ten leuvae in length and eight broad [207 km^2]. In the time of Edward the Confessor it was valued at eight marks of silver [£5.33]; now at forty shillings [£2.00].*

In Attercliffe and Sheffield, two manors, Sweyn had five carucates of land [~2.4 km^2] to be taxed. There may have been about three ploughs. This land is said to have been inland, demesne [domain] land of the manor of Hallam.

ST. PAUL'S CHURCH.

St Paul's Church that stood on the site of the Peace Gardens until its demolition in 1938

CHAPTER SEVENTEEN

Where to chill in 1862

With the factories going full pelt, the kids at work cleaning the chimneys and the majority of the town's working class housing a ramshackle disgrace, it was good to know Sheffield offered the odd bit of respite in the shape of the following recreation opportunities. Pawson & Brailsford recommended the following in their ground-breaking guide of 1862:

THE BOTANICAL GARDENS – *These gardens are amongst the most beautiful in the country. They are moreover situated in one of the most charming spots in the immediate vicinity of the town. They occupy about 18 acres of land between Clarkhouse-road and Ecclesall-road. They slope down towards the valley of the Porter, and from them may be seen, on the opposite hill-side, the picturesque grounds and the graceful church of the General Cemetery. The gardens were established by a company in 1836, at a total cost of about £18,000. They were at first a failure, and the original proprietors sold their interest in them to a new company for £9,000. Since that time the undertaking has, amidst many difficulties, gone on very prosperously. Though the property belongs to a company, it is not all carried on with a view to profit, but solely that the use of the gardens may be enjoyed by the town. They are admirably managed. There are large and handsome conservatories, spacious gardens tastefully laid out, with beautiful lawns, walks, grottoes, and arbours. During the summer "promenades" are periodically held. Upon these occasions music is provided, and the gardens are numerously attended by the leading inhabitants. Nor are the general public uncared for. Several galas are held in the course of every summer , when the price of admission is fixed at a low rate. Sometimes twenty or thirty thousand people crowd the place on these occasions. Constant access to the gardens is of course only permitted to shareholders and subscribers; but visitors from other towns can always obtain admission through a shareholder. The gardens are open the whole of every day except Sunday, when they are closed during the morning. Mr. Marshall, solicitor, Chapel-walk, Fargate, is secretary; and Mr. John Ewing, who resides at the gardens, is the curator.*

NORFOLK PARK - These are spacious pleasure grounds constantly open to the public, situated on the estates of the Duke of Norfolk, and which the town owes to the munificence of the grandfather of the present inheritor of the title. The park comprises altogether more than 60 acres. It has been laid out in ornamental walks, carriage drives, &c., and is well planted with shrubs and trees. In the centre there is a large open space covered with grass, which is used for cricket matches, &c. Here also has been held for some years past a poultry show on a large scale. Very beautiful views of the surrounding scenery are to be obtained from various spots in Norfolk Park.

THEATRE ROYAL – This building is situated at the corner of Arundel-street and Tudor-street. It belongs to a company of proprietors. It is a spacious edifice and very commodious. It was erected in 1773. In 1855 it was re-opened, after having been entirely rebuilt except the outer walls, at a cost of about £3,000. The re-construction of the general edifice was carried out by Messers. Flockton and Sons, of Sheffield, and that of the stage by Mr. Straughan, of London. When these alterations were adopted, many modern improvements were introduced. Since that time other changes have been made, the result of which is a commodious and elegant building. It is at present under the lesseeship of Mr. Charles Pitt.

CRICKET GROUNDS, &c. – There are two public cricket grounds. One is in Bramall-lane, and was opened in 1855. It cost (without land) nearly £3,000. It is commodious and well kept: the entire extent is more than eight acres. The other cricket ground is at Hyde-park. Norfolk-park is also used as a cricket ground. There are three bowling greens kept up by annual subscription, one in Broomgrove-road, another at the Bramall-lane cricket ground, and the third at Pitsmoor. There are three football clubs, the Sheffield, the Pitsmoor, and the Hallam. In connection with these there are annual sports and athletic games, which, especially those of the Sheffield Club, are attended by the elite of the town. There is also a Racket Club in Tudor-street.

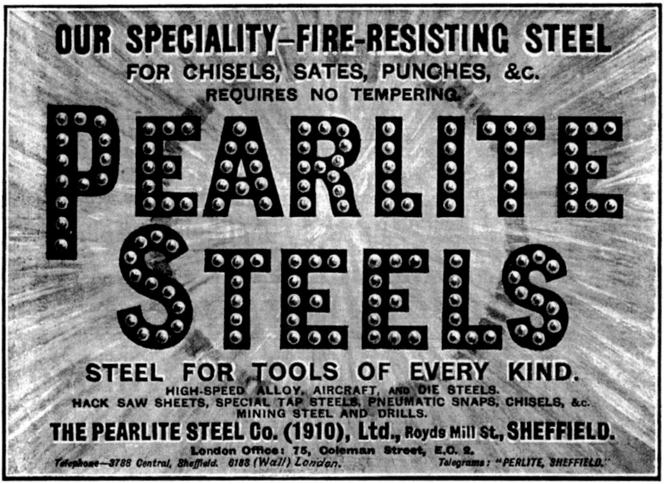

THE

WHARNCLIFFE,

KING-ST., SHEFFIELD.

The Proprietors respectfully announce completion of alterations, with a view to the further requirements and comfort of the Public.

THE ARRANGEMENTS IN

THE BUFFET

Now offer selections of PORTS and SHERRIES of the Finest Quality, drawn from the Wood, and supplied in Dock Glasses, at very moderate prices.

THE NEW

SMOKING, READING AND WRITING ROOM,

On the Ground Floor, is abundantly provided with DAILY and WEEKLY JOURNALS, and has a CIGAR CABINET, containing over Twenty Brands of the Finest Havana Tobacco. Coffee instantly served at any hour. Entrance through the Hall.

THE RESTAURANT,

Replete with every convenience, affords great facilities to Families, Residents, Commercial Gentlemen, and other Visitors to the Town.

THE HOTEL ACCOMMODATION

Is of a first-class character, and Guests are assured that nothing is spared to promote their comfort and satisfaction.

WM. H. GARSIDE, Manager.

CHAPTER EIGHTEEN

Fast facts

Sheffield – derives its name from the River Sheaf which runs through the city.

Nickname: 'Steel City'. Informally known as 'the biggest village in England'.

Motto: "Deo Adjuvante Labor Proficit' ('With God's Help Our Labour Is Successful').

It has the world's oldest football club in the shape of Sheffield FC (formed in 1857) – its Hallam FC follows closely as the second.

A third of Sheffield falls within the boundary of the Peak National Park.

Sheffield Town Hall is a Grade 1 listed building that was opened in 1897 by Queen Victoria. It has a 210 foot tower with a bronze figure of Vulcan, the God of Fire, standing at its peak.

TENNANT BROTHERS,

ALE, PORTER AND BITTER BEER

Brewers,

Exchange Brewery,

BRIDGE STREET,

SHEFFIELD.

☞ *Also Brewers of Beer for Export.*

CHAPTER NINETEEN

Sheffield - football city

Sheffield is the undisputed birthplace of world football and the scene of many of the game's most important landmark happenings.

Sheffield FC, the world's oldest club, was founded on October 24, 1857.

The city produced the first rule book.

In 1866 Sheffield took part in the first inter-city match, against London, and regular Sheffield-London matches led to the launch of the FA Cup, the world's oldest soccer competition.

1868 saw a whistle used by a referee for the first time in a match between Sheffield Norfolk and Nottingham Forest.

The world's first floodlit match took place at Sheffield's Bramall Lane on October 14, 1878, watched by 20,000.

In 1898 the first Charity Shield was contested between Sheffield United and the Corinthians, and SUFC also figured in the first broadcast match of 1927.

Sheffield Wednesday, the fifth oldest club in the football league, was founded in 1867, and Sheffield United was founded in 1889.

EXCHANGE DRAPERY CO.

LIMITED,

Victoria Buildings,

Fargate, Sheffield.

(Late GRAYS AND HENDERSON.)

PARIS & LONDON MILLINERY

BONNETS & HATS.

ENGLISH AND FRENCH

FLOWERS, FEATHERS, RIBBONS.

REAL AND IMITATION LACES.

SEWN MUSLINS.

LADIES' UNDER-CLOTHING.

BABY-LINEN.

DRESS AND MANTLE TRIMMINGS.

Haberdashery.

HOSIERY AND GLOVES.

GENTLEMEN'S OUTFITTING.

FURS.

UMBRELLAS AND SUNSHADES.

FRENCH AND SPITALFIELDS

Silk, Silk Velvets, and Velveteens.

BONNET MATERIALS.

MANTLES, JACKETS.

SHAWLS, SKIRTS.

PLAIN AND FANCY

DRESS MATERIALS.

COSTUMES.

EXPERIENCED

DRESS-MAKERS AND MILLINERS

ON THE PREMISES.

MOURNING & SPECIAL ORDERS

EXECUTED PROMPTLY.

LINENS, CALICOS, SHEETINGS, QUILTS, BLANKETS, CURTAINS, &c.

DAMASKS. WOOLLEN CLOTHS.

Mourning Department.

Crapes, French Merinos, Paramattas, Baratheas, Alpacas, Coburgs, &c.

ALL GOODS MARKED IN PLAIN FIGURES.

CHAPTER TWENTY

Did you know?

Harry Houdini learnt one of his most famous escapism tricks in an attic in Sheffield's suburb of Ecclesall.

Sheffield department store Atkinsons had its own bomb proof safe installed to be ready for Hitler in WW2. Unfortunately the member of staff on duty on the night of the Sheffield Blitz forgot to shut the door and everything inside it, including details of every penny owed to the store by customers, was destroyed.

Sheffield Wednesday started out as 'The Wednesday Cricket Club' (named after the day they played) in 1820. The football team was formed to keep them fit in the winter.

Sheffield's role was pivotal to the Battle of Britain. It was home to the only drop hammer in the country that could make the Merlin crankshafts for the Spitfire.

Though Elvis Presley never performed in the UK, Sheffield probably came closer than anyone to landing him. All conquering seventies venue, The Fiesta, were eager to hold a date open for him and calls from the star's manager were regularly intercepted by the venue's switchboard .

Double Sheffield Portrait

She owned him lock, stock and barrel.
She owned the trousers that depended from his shanks.
She owned the gloves that muffled his creaky fingers.
She owned every last part of him, with small thanks.

She owned him lock, stock and barrel.
She owned his whistle, reedy, across the pond.
She owned the saliva in his mouth, and the roaring
in his chest.
She owned the busyness of his words,
and his small and finicky infuriations.
She owned the pots and pans that hung amidst
the tools in his dank and lonely shed.
She owned his life, such as it was.

He owned her, lock, stock and barrel.
He owned how she glared at him long and long,
ike motor car headlights left on in the night.

He owned the gristle in her voice, and the stamp
of her ungainly hoof.
He owned her buttocks, her ears, those tufty sprigs
that showered out from each ear.
He owned every last part of her, and he made of her
what he could.

Michael Glover – from 'Only So Much', 2011

About the author

Neil Anderson has been amassing Sheffield-related trivia for nigh on 20 years and despite writing five books about the city and its history, there was still a lot more waiting for a home.

'Facts, Figures and Fallacious Goings-On In Sheffield' is that home.

Neil Anderson was a Sheffield Telegraph columnist for over a decade and has written for newspapers spanning The Independent to the Yorkshire Post.

When he's not writing books he's running media relations company All Credit Media (www.allcreditmedia.com) and publishing company ACM Retro (www.acmretro.com).

Acknowledgements:

Sheffield Archives, Local Studies Library, Sheffield Newspapers, Dave Manvell, BBC Radio Sheffield, Michael Glover, Maggie Soutar, Geoff Rowe, Jethro Soutar, Marie Jenkinson, John and Linda Mitchell and Hallamshire Historic Buildings Society (www.hhbs.org.uk).

Proofing - Lindsay McLaren, Ian Cheetham and Peter Eales

Balancing the books – Ian Cheetham

Layout - Karen Davies

All round inspiration – Lowri and Ewan Anderson

Inspiration and loathing of Sheffieldisms – Lindsay McLaren

References:

Anderson, Neil (2009) *Shopaholics Guide to 1970s Sheffield*: Sheffield: ACM Retro

Anderson, Neil (2009) *Take It To The Limit*: Sheffield: ACM Retro

Anderson, Neil (2010) *Sheffield's Date With Hitler*: Sheffield: ACM Retro

Bentley, David (2002) *The Sheffield Hanged 1750-1864*: Sheffield: ALD

Bunker, Bessie (1972) *Portrait of Sheffield*: London: Robert Hale

Glinert & Perry (1997) Rock And Roll Traveller Great Britain and Ireland: Fodor's

Harrison, Samuel (1864) *A Complete History of The Great Flood at Sheffield*: Evans and Longley Associates

Morning Telegraph (1972) *Sheffield Year Book And Industrial Directory 1972-1973*: Sheffield: Sheffield Newspapers Limited

Pawson & Brailsford (1879) *Illustrated Guide to Sheffield*: Sheffield: Pawson and Brailsford

Pawson & Brailsford(1862) *Illustrated Guide to Sheffield:* Sheffield: Pawson and Brailsford

Vickers, Edward (1978) *A Popular History of Sheffield*: Sheffield: Applebaum

Wormersley, Derek (1981) *"Sheffieldish" A Beginner's Phrase-Book*: Sheffield: Sheffield City Council